AUTUMN

A collection of
Poems, Songs and Stories
for young children

**Wynstones
Press**

Published by
Wynstones Press
Stourbridge
England.
Email: info@wynstonespress.com
Website: www.wynstonespress.com

First Published 1978 by Wynstones Press
Second edition with music 1983
Fully revised third edition 1999. Reprinted 2005, 2010, 2015.

Editors: Jennifer Aulie and Margret Meyerkort

Cover illustration of 'The Blacksmith' by David Newbatt

Typeset by Wynstones Press.
Printed in EU.

British Library CIP data available.

ISBN 9780 946206 483

Autumn

This is one in a series of 6 books:
Spring, Summer, Autumn, Winter, Spindrift and Gateways.

The four seasonal books comprise a wide selection of poems, songs and stories appropriate to the time of year, including much material for the celebration of festivals.

Spindrift contains verses and songs describing the world of daily work and practical life, together with a selection of stories from around the world.

Gateways comprises verses and songs for the Morning time, the Evening time and to accompany a variety of traditional Fairytales, together with poems, songs and stories for the celebration of Birthdays.

Warmest thanks to all who have contributed to and supported this work: parents, teachers and friends from Steiner Waldorf Schools in Australia, Britain, Canada, Eire, Estonia, New Zealand, Norway, South Africa and the United States. Grateful thanks also to publishers who have permitted the use of copyright material, acknowledgements for which are at the end of the volume.

INDEX

Indexes of first lines
POEMS

SONGS

Index of titles
STORIES

The Value of Music in the Life of the Young Child

Free Play in a Waldorf Kindergarten. It is a winter morning: the twenty children are busy with their work. The youngest, three- and four-year-olds, are helping the teacher chop apples for snack; some five-year-old girls are taking care of their "children" in the doll corner; next to them are a group of five-year-old boys and girls who are sitting at a round table polishing stones, grating chestnuts and chatting together. In the centre of the room an observant and energetic four-year-old boy is directing the six-year-olds in the construction of a snowplough: tables are stacked on each other, chairs turned upside down and leaned against the tables for the front part of the plough. A large basket of chestnuts is balanced on top of the plough. The chestnuts are grit and salt, to be scattered later on the ploughed streets. The room is small and the noise level is moderately high.

Underneath the windows, on the carpet where the children have a free space to build up scenes and play with standing puppets and animals, a six-year-old girl sits, absorbed in her work. She has laid out a forest of pine cones, which stands on the banks of a river of blue cloth. Stepping stones allow the poor shepherd boy, who lives at the edge of the forest, to cross the river and wind his way to the castle gates nearby . . . The princess, leaning out of her tower, sees him coming and calls down to him . . .

As she lays out the scene, the girl accompanies her actions with narrative, speaking in a soft tone, sometimes almost whispering to herself. When the puppets begin to live in the scene her voice changes, becoming more sung than spoken, the pitch of her spoken voice being taken over by her singing voice. Her recitative is not sing-song rhythmic, but the rhythm freely moves with the intention of the shepherd boy as he jumps from stone to stone. The pitch of the girl's voice is a colourful monotone: the pitch remains much the same, but the tone colour is enlivened through the intensity and quality of the words as the shepherd crosses the stream. There are moments when a word is spoken, then the narrative is sung again.

When the shepherd arrives at the castle gates, the princess calls down to him from her high tower. She is far away, and the girl reaches up with her voice to the distant place where the princess lives, and sings her greetings down to the shepherd. The girl's voice is high now, but the intervals she sings are not large, they are between a third and a fifth. The high pitch of her voice, although it is not loud, has attracted some of the five-year-olds: several come over to the rug and lie on their stomachs, watching the play unfold. The shepherd now tells the princess of his wish that she come down and go with him. The simple recitative changes to a declamatory aria: a melody of several different tones arises, moving stepwise, the girl's voice becomes more intense as the shepherd pleads his cause. There is little repetition in the melody, but the movement contained in it provides a musical mood which waits expectantly for the princess's reply . . .

In the meantime, the snowplough has already cleared quite a few streets. It has come back to make a second round to scatter the grit and salt . . . The four-year-olds slicing apples jump up from the table. The noise of all those chestnuts hitting a wooden floor is so wonderful, they want to join the fun! The "mothers" putting their children to bed are angry that the snowplough has woken up their little ones, now the babies are crying . . . Some of the children polishing stones and grating chestnuts try throwing their stones and chestnuts on the floor – what a good idea, it makes a lovely *cracking* sound . . .

. . . the five-year-olds listening to the play hold their breaths as the princess agrees to go with the shepherd but he must first ask permission from her father, the king . . . The princess's instructions are sung to him in a melody of seconds with a strong, definite rhythm . . .

An observer can hardly believe that the chestnut-strewn chaos in the other half of the room (which the teacher is quickly helping to put right again) does not seem to penetrate the sheath of peacefulness which surrounds the puppet play. The children gathered around it show no sign that anything else in the room has taken place . . .

At the successful conclusion of the play, the children watching it lie still. The girl covers the scene with a cloth and sings in a half-whispering tone a farewell to the story of the shepherd and the princess. As her voice fades, there is a moment of absolute silence. Then the five-year-olds run back to the polishing table and the girl goes to the teacher to ask how long it will be until snack.

This description of a six-year-old girl's singing contains many elements of what has come to be called "Mood of the Fifth" music: the singing follows the rhythm of speech; melodies are simple, moving within intervals of seconds and thirds – sometimes as large as a fifth, rarely larger; melodies are often sung on one tone, the pitch taken from the speaking voice; the melodies are not written in major or in minor keys and have an open-ended feel to them. Above all is the mood of the music: when sung properly it seems to reach out and enfold the children in a protective sheath which has a quality of stillness and peace, although the children themselves may be active within it.

This music is a musical expression of an experience which is striven for in all aspects of Waldorf Education. It is difficult to describe in words, perhaps: "I am centred in my activity," "My thinking, feeling and willing are in balance." One feels deeply united with a task, at peace and yet still active. The young child finds this mood in play. S/he is deeply engaged in an activity which is then no longer interesting when the activity is over. The moment of silence at the end of the play was not a moment of reflection, but a moment which allowed the activity of watching the play to come to a complete end before the next task could engage the children's attention.

The broader context of this musical experience should be noted: the kindergarten just described is one where mood-of-the-fifth music was not cultivated by the teacher. The children learned only traditional children's songs and games which were sung in strict rhythm, and with major or minor key melodies. The six-year-old girl experienced similar music at home.

Yet the girl's singing is not an isolated or unusual musical event. Such singing can often be heard when a child's attention is fully engaged in his/her play. We grown-ups tend to dismiss such fragments of melody as noise, or incomplete attempts by the child to sing our music, not listening closely enough to discover the innate coherence of the child's activity. Too often well-meaning adults try to "correct" the pitch which is too high, or the rhythm which is irregular, and slowly wall in a living musicality with "proper" songs . . . Sooner or later, often at puberty, an attempt is made at breaking through these walls, as the pounding beat of popular music has long suggested.

The use of "Mood of the Fifth" music in the kindergarten encompasses two considerations. It is first of all a path of musical development for the adult, which schools his/her musical perception and ability so that s/he is able to participate in a musicality which the children *already possess.* This musicality may, for many reasons, lie dormant or misshapen within an individual child or group of children. Through the adult's use of Mood of the Fifth s/he can reawaken and bring back into movement the musicality which is so essential for the full development of the child's soul life. (To be labelled "unmusical" or "tone deaf" causes deep, lingering wounds to the child's self esteem. There are unfortunately many adults who can attest to the truth of this statement out of their own experience.)

Mood of the Fifth music can also help the adult to establish an additional point of contact with the child which shows him/her that the adult *understands.* One of the rewards of working with young children is surely the open look of delight on a child's face when s/he hears a story, plays a game, experiences something which pleases him/her. The look of delight means more, however, than just "I like that." On a deeper level it expresses the child's trust in the adult: "You know who I am, and what you offer me is that which I am searching for with my deepest intentions. I can follow you."

The present day task of the Waldorf Kindergarten is primarily a therapeutic one. It provides children with basic experiences which they need for healthy development, overcoming deficiencies which often occur today in the first years of life. A very large part of these experiences are sensory, as the development of the physical senses (touch, balance, etc.) lays the foundation for the later unfolding of the spiritual capacities (thinking, speech, etc.). The kindergarten is not a mirror of our daily lives, but an extract of the many activities, distilled to their essence. This provides a simplicity and basic necessity for the content of kindergarten life which the child can understand and imitate wholeheartedly. The meaningful activity around the child awakens his/her interest in the world, and this interest becomes the mainspring of later learning.

In the arts the materials presented to the child are restricted to essentials, and with these the child's imagination has free rein. This can be clearly seen, for example, in painting: the three primary colours are used – red, yellow and blue. The children are given watercolours, a large wet sheet of paper and a broad brush to paint with. The materials themselves preclude any precise drawing, colours flow into one another, sometimes mixing, sometimes remaining pure side by side. There is no right or wrong way of using the colours, the expansive, fiery or cool moods of the colours themselves guide the child's brush. The medium of water enables the child's soul to breathe freely in the movement of colour with the brush. If only the paper were bigger s/he could paint on and on . . .

Music can be approached in a similar way. Here as well the materials can be restricted so that the *activity* becomes of foremost importance. Only five different tones of our twelve tone system are used:

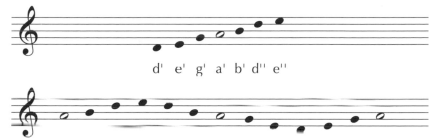

d' e' g' a' b' d'' e''

When a children's harp or lyre is used, the strings are tuned to pure fifths (like a violin's open strings) rather than the tempered intervals of the piano. The songs are not written in major or minor keys, but tend to circle around the middle tone, a'. The rhythm is free, either gently swinging (3 or 6 beats) or walking (2 or 4 beats), but the movement of the music takes its impulse from the words and seeks to accompany its inner content.

This style of music making lends itself wonderfully to the activities of circle time where movement, the spoken word and song freely flow from one to the other, just as the three basic colours do in painting. Teachers who have worked with Mood of the Fifth music in the classroom also know of its effectiveness in creating moments where the attention of all of the children is engaged, enabling a special mood to arise, whether in a puppet play, grace before meal, etc.

Newcomers to this music may at first experience difficulty in hearing the melodies or finding an inner connection to them. Others may have trouble finding the beginning pitch or singing the songs as high as they are written. None of these difficulties should be considered unsolvable problems.

Over time, the practice of Music of the Fifth songs often leads to a good sense of pitch. The voice gradually learns the placement of the tones, and the reduced number of tones make sight-singing possible even for the "unmusical" person.

Difficulty in reaching the higher notes (d", e"), which lie within traditional singing range of soprano and altos, can be due to breathing which is too shallow, as well as to the false idea that high notes are more difficult to sing and require greater effort. In the long run, the question of extending the vocal range is best addressed by an experienced teacher. But those without a teacher can still consider the following: the vocal range can be affected by physical movement. Often much can be accomplished by accompanying a song with large, simple, physical gestures. This helps free the breathing, allowing greater ease in reaching notes which are "too high." The songs can be practised with movement until the feeling of vocal mobility is secure. Then the outward movement can gradually become smaller and disappear altogether, all the while maintaining the inner freedom of movement in the voice.

An essential guide for adults who wish to find a path into the experience of Mood of the Fifth music can be found in Julius Knierim's *Songs in the Mood of the Fifth (Quintenlieder)*. This succinct and clearly written booklet describes, with simple exercises and musical examples, a path which really can be taken by all who have a sincere interest in further development of their musical abilities. By working with the suggestions contained in Julius Knierim's essay, the serious student can develop capacities which not only lead him/her into the musical world of the young child, but can help build a new relationship to traditional classical music, and even to music of this century.

Rudolf Steiner, in discussing music for the young child, spoke of the great importance of the Quintenstimmung = *Mood* of the Fifth. The suggestions mentioned in this article, and most especially in Dr. Knierim's book, are guideposts by which adults may find the way into this mood. They are not the mood itself. Individual observation, experimentation, and practice are the means by which the letter of the law may be enlivened by its spirit.

The goal of these booklets is to offer immediate practical help in working with young children. It is for this reason that a variety of musical styles is included. All songs (as well as stories and verses) have proved their worth in Waldorf kindergartens or other settings with young children. Some traditional tunes with new words have been included, and many traditional rhymes have been set to new melodies (either pentatonic or Mood of the Fifth). Familiar children's songs have been excluded for the most part because these are readily available in other collections. Most songs are set in D-pentatonic. This is done for pedagogical as well as practical reasons (see references). Experience has shown that many teachers and parents who wish to consciously address music-making with the young child are often just those who are themselves struggling with their own musical education. With most songs written in D-pentatonic mode (which are tones of a Choroi flute or children's harp, and are easy to play on a traditional recorder), it is hoped that the initial difficulties with note reading and transposition will be eased. The use of bar lines and time signatures varies, showing new possibilities of notation. Some songs have traditional time signatures, others have only a 3 or 4 at the beginning to indicate a more swinging or walking rhythm. The absence of bar lines leaves the singer free to determine the musical phrasing according to the rhythm of the words and their sense. Commas indicate a slight pause, or point of rest.

Jennifer Aulie

References:

Knierim, Julius. *Songs in the Mood of the Fifth 'Quintenlieder'*.
ISBN 0 945803 14 1 (Rudolf Steiner College Press, California)

Steiner, Rudolf. *The Study of Man*.
ISBN 9781855841871 (Rudolf Steiner Press, England)

Steiner, Rudolf. *The Inner Nature of Music and the Experience of Tone*.
ISBN 9780880100748 (Steiner Books, USA)

M. Meyerkort

M. Meyerkort   *N. Foster*

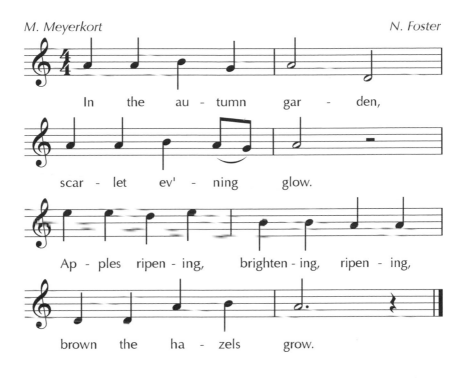

In the au - tumn gar - den,

scar - let ev' - ning glow.

Ap - ples ripen - ing, brighten - ing, ripen - ing,

brown the ha - zels grow.

M. Meyerkort   *N. Foster*

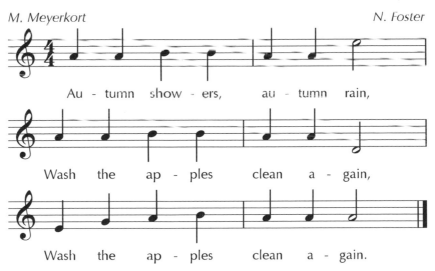

Au - tumn show - ers, au - tumn rain,

Wash the ap - ples clean a - gain,

Wash the ap - ples clean a - gain.

G. Sargeant

N. Foster

Fa - ther Sky, Fa - ther Sky, wide - ly lov - ing

blue and high, wide - ly lov - ing blue and high.

Mo-ther Earth your warm-ing glow makes the corn and

ap - ples grow, makes the corn and ap - ples grow.

C. Comeras

The har - vest time a - gain is here for

all both far and near. It is the time we

ga - ther food to last us all the year.

F. Hoatson

P. Patterson

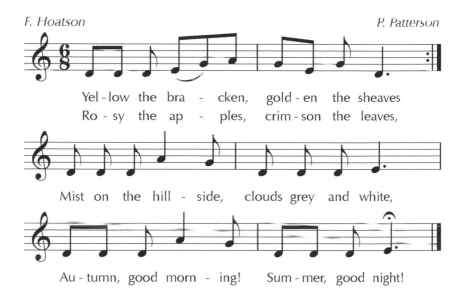

Yel - low the bra - cken, gold - en the sheaves
Ro - sy the ap - ples, crim - son the leaves,

Mist on the hill - side, clouds grey and white,

Au - tumn, good morn - ing! Sum - mer, good night!

M. Meyerkort

C. Comeras

Bind the bar - ley in - to bales,

tie ____ the string to - ge - ther,

Lift the corn on - to the cart,

all in the au - tumn wea - ther.

M. Meyerkort   P. Patterson

I - ron   bright,   cut   with   might!

Sun   and   moon   and   star   and   earth

Brought   the   gold - en   corn   to   birth.

I - ron   bright,   cut   with   might!

   2. Mill, oh mill, on the hill,
      Turn your wings with all your might,
      Grind the corn to flour white.
      Mill, oh mill, on the hill.

   1. Pull the cart, my pony, pull,
      Careful for the cart is full.
      To the miller take your road,
      Slowly with this heavy load.

   2. Pull the cart, my donkey, pull,
      Careful for the cart is full.
      To the baker take your road,
      Slowly with this heavy load.

M. Meyerkort

1. Swing your scythe, Oh swing away,
   Mow the corn, 'tis harvest day.

2. Bind the barley, bind away,
   Tie the string, 'tis harvest day.

3. Hammer, hammer, knock away,
   Thresh the corn, 'tis harvest day.

4. Turn the wheel, Oh turn away,
   Grind the corn, 'tis harvest day.

5. Knead the dough, Oh knead away,
   Bake the bread, 'tis harvest day.

M. Meyerkort

Oh I'm a jolly miller, hey, and I work with a will.
The wild winds whirl around and round the sails of my mill.
Make the bonny breezes blow,
That around and around they go,
For my sack I cannot fill
If they stand all stock and still.

Blow, wind, blow!
Go, mill, go!
That the miller may grind his corn.
Then the baker will take it
And into bread make it
And bring us a loaf in the morn.

Now is the time our harvest to reap,
To gather the corn sheaves into a heap,
To thrash with great vigour, we'll sing and we'll laugh,
As we separate corn seeds away from the chaff.
Then off to the windmill with corn that is good,
To grind and make bread that man may have food.

Swing your sickle
Swing again.
Downward falling
Goes the grain.

Miller, miller, meet the farmer
When the weather has turned warmer.

Buy his wheat and stack it till
You shall take it to the mill.

Windmill, windmill, turn around
Never stop till the wheat is ground.

Baker, baker, hurry and go
To the bakehouse, bake your dough.

Oven, oven, cook your bread
That the children all are fed.

Oven, oven, see that you bake
An icy, spicy, sugary cake.

A sugary cake, a loaf of bread,
And so the children will be fed.

I. O. Eastwick

When the wind blows,
Then the mill goes.
When the wind drops,
Then the mill stops.
Clickety – clackety,
Clickety – clackety,
Clickety – clackety,
Clickety – clack.

Look across the green and grassy hill,
You can see the farmer's busy mill;
How the wind with whistling sound
Moves the long arms round and round!

From France

1. Ho! To be a farmer and to walk behind my plough!
    To feed the little chickens and to milk the mooly cow!
    To tell the good horse, Dobbin, how to "haw" and "gee"
    Ho! To be a farmer, that's the life for me!

2. Ho! To be a farmer and to bring the harvest in!
    To stack the hay and cut the corn and put it in the bin!
    The winter storms will find me cosy as can be.
    Ho! To be a farmer, that's the life for me!

A. Riley

Farmer, is the harvest ready,
For we must have bread?
Go and look at all my fields,
Is what the farmer said.

So we ran and saw the wheat
Standing straight and tall.
There's your wheat, the farmer said,
Have no fear at all.

Miller, is the flour ready,
For we must have bread?
Go and look in all my sacks,
Is what the miller said.

So we ran and saw the flour
Soft and white as snow.
There's your flour, the miller said,
As we turned to go.

Mother, is the oven ready,
For we must have bread?
Go and open wide the door,
Is what our mother said.

So we ran and saw the loaves
Crisp and brown to see.
There's your bread, our mother said,
Ready for your tea.

H. E. Wilkinson

1. Come, old Dobbin, not so slow,
   We have many miles to go;
   There are corn and oats and hay
   In the barn for you today.

2. We are coming back from town,
   Past the fields, uphill and down;
   Now we're nearing home once more,
   I can see the old barn door.

   C. Crane

THE HARVEST

The silver rain, the shining sun,
The fields where scarlet poppies run,
And all the ripples of the wheat
Are in the bread that we do eat.

So when we sit for every meal
And say a grace: we always feel
That we are eating rain and sun,
And fields where scarlet poppies run.

   A. Henderson

A farmer rose at the break of day,
He got on his horse and he galloped away.
He galloped away, he galloped away,
He got on his horse and he galloped away.
Oh, come all my men, oh come, said he,
Our carrots and turnips for to see.
In the warm brown earth they have grown so big
We must bring out our spades and dig and dig.
So fetch your spades and come along
To dig up the roots with your arms so strong,
To lay them out in the sun to dry,
And then in the cart pile them up on high.

GNOME KING

Good friends, you have more work to do,
For yonder on the earth I know
Summer is fading and the winds do blow.
Your next task is with seeds so small,
To see them safely in this hall,
Away from Jack Frost who would do them harm.
My Queen and I await them.

S. Jarman

Trip, trip, trap, trip, trip, trap,
Go the gnomes along their track,
Heaving up upon their backs,
Gold and silver in their sacks.
Now through caverns dark and drear,
We make our way to our king so dear.
Down we go to the throne of our king,
To him our treasures we must bring.

S. Jarman

Through echoing caverns we run and we glide,
Through cracks in the rocks we slip and we slide,
Over great boulders we leap and we bound,
Our little lamps show us where treasures are found.
We hammer, we hammer from morning till night,
We hammer to gather the treasures so bright:
Sparkling silver and glittering gold,
Crystals so pure and so clean to behold.
Then up we fill our little sacks
And raise them high upon our backs.
Down we will go to the throne of our King,
To him our treasures we all must bring.
Soon, soon,
By the light of the moon,
We build the crystal mirror bright,
The stones shall shed their golden light
On sleeping seeds in the earth tonight.

GNOMES

Oh! Look at our lanterns,
They cheerily shine,
Come follow their bright golden ray.
The king and queen await you,
For they will now protect you
And guard you from all harm.
Then as the days do lengthen,
For new growth they will strengthen,
And set you on your way.
So sleep little seeds the long winter through,
Sink quickly and gently to rest.

S. Jarman

27

Gnomes: Little seeds, now look out,
Jack Frost is about.
Oh, come now to dear Mother Earth.
She will keep you so warm
And guard you from harm,
Till the spring sun gives you new birth.

Seeds: So dark is the path,
How it twists and turns!
Oh shall we not lose our way?

Gnomes: No, look, our lanterns
They cheerily shine,
Come follow their bright, golden way.

Seeds: Now down we all come
To dear Mother Earth,
She will teach us to sleep on her breast.

Gnomes: So sleep, little seeds all the cold winter long,
Sink quietly, gently to rest.

G. Sargeant

D. Hancock   *D. Hancock*

We car-ry our light in the dark-en-ing night, That

we may be-hold that wond - rous sight.

S. Czemmel

S. Czemmel

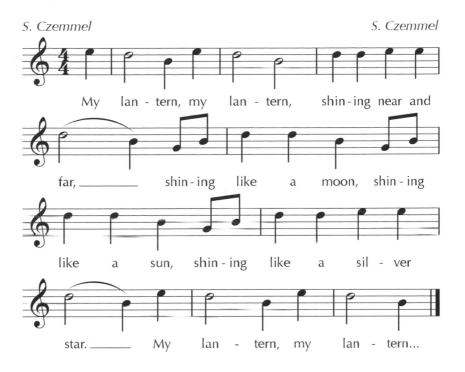

My lan-tern, my lan-tern, shin-ing near and far, _____ shin-ing like a moon, shin-ing like a sun, shin-ing like a sil-ver star. _____ My lan-tern, my lan-tern...

M. Meyerkort

N. Foster

The sun-light fast is dwind-ling, My lit-tle lamp needs kind-ling, Its beam shines far in dark-est night, Dear lan-tern, guard me with your light.

From Germany   M. Garff

Glim - mer, lan - tern, glim - mer, Lit - tle stars a -

shim - mer. O - ver mea - dow, moor and dale,

Flit - ter flut - ter elf - in veil. Pee - wit, pee - wit,

Tick - a - tick - a - tick, Roo - coo, roo - coo.

2. Glimmer, lantern, glimmer,
    Little stars a-shimmer.
    Over rock and stock and stone,
    Wander tripping little gnome.
    Pee-witt, pee-witt,
    Tick-a-tick-a-tick,
    Roo-coo, roo-coo.

The boughs do shake, the bells do ring,
So merrily comes our harvest in,
Our harvest in, our harvest in,
So merrily comes our harvest in.

We have ploughed, we have sowed,
We have reaped, we have mowed,
We have brought home every load.
Hip, hip, hip, harvest home.

P. R. Chalmers

P. Patterson

When Ma - ry goes walk - ing the au - tumn winds blow, The pop - lars they curt - sey, the larch - es bow low, The oaks and the beech - es their gold they fling down, To make her a car - pet, to make her a crown.

31

P. Baumann   P. Baumann

Wind in wood, blow, ___ blow,

all the leaves are rust - ling.

Sing a song of au - tumn leaves

as the trees bend high and low.

Wind in wood blow, ___ blow,

all the leaves are rust - ling.

2. Michaël, angel bright,
   Flaming sword is guiding,
   Sing a song of twinkling stars
   As they sparkle in the night.
   Michaël, angel bright
   Flaming sword is guiding.

Verse 2: J. Marcus.

32

Here stand we, strong, brave and free!
All nature's children fall asleep.
Man alone the watch can keep,
So we must watchful be!
For we know a secret old,
Precious more than gems and gold,
That in darkest winter night
We may seek the Christ Child's light.

D. Hancock.

M. L. Channer   *M. L. Channer*

I am Mi - cha - ël's help - er,
I am Mi - cha - ël's help - er,

Like his light shin - ing bright, I
Like his lyre sound - ing clear, I

come to you.
come to you.

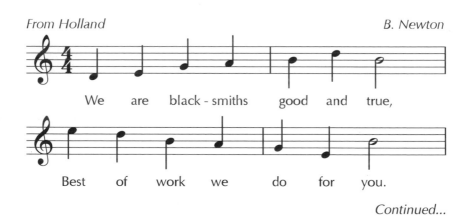

Continued...

Can you work with one ham - mer,

Clang - ing, clang - ing, clang - ing, so? With a

rik - ker - de, tik - ker - de, tik - ker - de tik, With a

rik - ker - de, tik - ker - de, tik - ker - de tik.

Suggested directions:

1. *One hammer: For the first two lines walk around in open circle formation. On the third line raise the right hand. On the fifth and sixth lines pat the right hand on the right thigh rhythmically.*

2. *Two hammers: Raise both hands on line 3, then both hands on thighs on lines 5 and 6.*

3. *Three hammers: On lines 5 and 6, the right hand on the right thighs with the left foot on the floor at the same time, alternating with the left hand on the left thigh.*

4. *Four hammers: The right hand and right foot together, alternating with the left hand and left foot together.*

A. Gladstone   P. Patterson

Soft - ly tread on si - lent toe,

Down from heav'n to earth we go:

Blue and pur - ple, gold and red,

Soft - ly tread, oh, soft - ly tread.

It's golden in the tree tops
It's golden in the sky,
It's golden, golden, golden,
September passing by.

I shake the trees
And blow my tune,
Ho, ho – the leaves
Will be dancing soon.

1. Pray, Sir Robin Redbreast, pray who gave you leave
   Cherries from my cherry tree thus to come and thieve?
   Pray you, sir, how is it yours?
   Did you make the tree?
   Can you prove those cherries, sir, don't belong to me?

2. Look, Sir Robin Redbreast, here I own the soil,
   And this tree I've planted here, tended it with toil.
   I help keep it free from worms.
   I have labour'd too.
   So I think the fruit belongs both to me and you.

3. Well, Sir Robin Redbreast, what you say is true.
   Eat your fill and never think I begrudge it you.
   Thank you very kindly, sir!
   Thanks to you I'll sing,
   And return to visit you early ev'ry Spring.

A. Riley

Oh, I wish me a galloping horse for to ride
And a helmet of gold and a sword at my side.
To the mountain I ride with a hey and a ho,
Against the old giant to battle I'll go.
Then I draw out my sword for a blow
And I drive the old giant below.
Now my pony, my pony, a-galloping go,
Let us ride to my home with a hey and a ho,
And my mother awaits me and smiles with delight
And she brings me a basket of red roses bright.

From Germany

W. J. Gerst

L. Clemm

In the fields, gold - en morn,

In - di - an child - ren ga - ther corn.

Chorus

Dance to the sun, dance to the rain,

dance to the earth who gives us grain.

Verse 2

In - di - an child - ren put fea - thers in their hair.

In - di - an child - ren string beads to wear.

Continued...

38

Verse 3

In - di - an child - ren walk as soft - ly as the deer,

To the te - pee with the gold - en ear.

Verse 4

A lit - tle fire they will make,

Bread of gold - en corn they will bake.

Verse 5

Bread of gold - en corn they'll eat, Then

In - di - an child - ren fall fast a - sleep.

The chorus is to be sung after each verse.

R. Fyleman

P. Patterson

Spin-dle wood, spin-dle wood, will you lend me,
pray, A lit-tle flam-ing lan-tern to
light me on my way? The fair-y folk have
van-ished from the mea-dow and the glen, And
I would fain go seek-ing till I find them once a-
gain. Oh, lend me now a lan-tern that
I may bear a light, To find the hid-den
path-way in the dark-ness of the night.

2. Ash tree, ash tree, throw me, if you please,
   Throw me down a slender bunch of russet-gold keys;
   I fear the gates of fairyland may all be shut fast;
   Give me of your magic keys that I may get past;
   I'll tie them to my girdle, that as I go along
   My heart may find a comfort in their tiny tinkling song.

3. Holly bush, holly bush, help me in my task,
   A pocketful of berries is all the alms I ask;
   A pocketful of berries to thread in glowing strands
   (I would not go a-visiting with nothing in my hands);
   So fine will be the rosy chains, so good, so glossy bright,
   They'll set the realms of fairyland a-dancing with delight.

THE LEAVES ARE GREEN

Sing to tune of 'Here we go round the mulberry bush.'
Everyone reaches up for apples, then all fall down!
The tune is on page 63 of Spindrift

1. The leaves are green, the apples are red,
   They hang so high above your head,
   Leave them alone till frosty weather
   Then they will all fall down together!

2. The leaves are green and the nuts are brown,
   They hang so high, and will not come down.
   Leave them alone till the frosty weather
   Then they will all come down together!

41

J. Aulie

Au-tumn has come to the coun-try and town,

Wear-ing its gar-ment of gold-en and brown.

Ap-ples she brings us so round and so red,

Brings us our corn that we bake our bread.

2. Lo, there's a bridge of wonderful light,
   Built of colours so warm and so bright,
   Brown, gold and purple and yellow and red,
   Softly we tread, then, so softly we tread.

J. Aulie

Verse 1: Ro - sy ap - ple, mel - low pear, Bunch of ros - es she shall wear, Gold and sil - ver by her side, I know who shall be my bride.

Verse 2: Take her by the li - ly white hand, Lead her 'cross the wa - ter, Give her kiss - es one, two, three, She's a la - dy's daugh ter.

Suggested directions:

A circle of children walks around, while 2 to 6 children stand in the centre. The circle stands still, and the centre children each choose a child from the circle.

2nd verse: Circle children raise arms for the pairs to walk in and out, and at the end the pairs stand in the centre.

Here's a little apple tree.
I look up and I can see
Big red apples, ripe and sweet,
Beg red apples, good to eat!
Shake the little apple tree.
See the apples fall on me.
Here's a basket, big and round,
Pick the apples from the ground.
Here's an apple I can see,
I'll reach up. It's ripe and sweet.
That's the apple I will eat!

Here stands a tall apple tree.
Stand fast at root.
Bear well at top,
Pray, God send us a howling crop.
Every twig
Bear an apple big.
Every bough
Bear an apple now.
Hats full! Caps full!
Three score sacks full
Hurrah! Boys! Hurrah!

Let's go walking through the woods
On this windy autumn day,
Through the leaves, all red and gold,
Let us dance and sing and play.

From Germany   P. Patterson

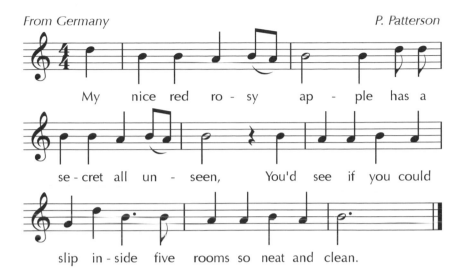

My   nice   red   ro - sy   ap - ple   has   a

se - cret   all   un - seen,   You'd   see   if   you   could

slip   in - side   five   rooms   so   neat   and   clean.

2. In each room there are living
   Two pips so black and bright,
   Asleep they are and dreaming
   Of lovely warm sunlight.

3. And sometimes they are dreaming
   Of many things to be,
   How soon they will be hanging
   Upon the Christmas tree.

1. Scarlet and yellow, golden and brown,
   Winds of October blow the leaves down.
   Tear from their branches their curtains and spread
   Carpets of yellow beneath them instead.

2. Glistening with rain or ablaze in the sun,
   Falling in showers or dropped one by one.
   Fluttering treasures of autumn come down,
   Scarlet and yellow and golden and brown.

S. Czemmel

Come lit - tle leaves, said the wind one day,

Come o'er the mea - dow with me to play,

Put on your dress - es of red and gold,

Sum - mer is gone and the days grow cold.

2. Soon as the leaves heard the wind's loud call,
   Down they came fluttering, one and all;
   Over the fields they danced and flew,
   Singing the soft little songs they knew.

3. Dancing and whirling the little leaves went
   Winter had called them, and they were content,
   Soon, fast asleep on their earthy bed,
   The snow laid a coverlet over their head.

Leaves are falling light, so light,
Yellow, red and brown.
Hedgehog finds a place to sleep,
Leaves his eiderdown.

S. Baines

C. Rossetti
J. Aulie

Who has seen the wind? Nei - ther I nor you, _____ But when the leaves hang tremb - ling down The wind is pass - ing through.

2. Who has seen the wind?
    Neither you nor I,
    But when the trees bow down their heads
    The wind is passing by.

THE SQUIRREL

Whisky, frisky, hoppity hop,
Up he goes to the tree top!
Whirly, twirly, round and round,
Down he scampers to the ground.
Furly, curly, what a tail!
Tall as a feather, broad as a sail!
Where's his supper? In the shell.
Snappity, crackity, out it fell.

These are the brown leaves
Fluttering down,
And this is the tall tree
Bare and brown.
This is the squirrel
With eyes so bright;
Hunting for nuts
With all his might.
This is the hole
Where day by day,
Nut after nut
He stores away.
When winter comes
With its cold and storm,
He'll sleep curled up
All snug and warm.

Grey squirrel, grey squirrel,
Swish your bushy tail.
Grey squirrel, grey squirrel,
Swish your bushy tail.
Wrinkle up your little nose,
Hold a nut between your toes.
Grey squirrel, grey squirrel,
Swish your bushy tail.

Up above the grey clouds rumble,
And in merry rush and tumble
Raindrops downwards dance and spatter,
Pitter patter, pitter patter.

S. Jarman

C. Glas   M. Meyerkort

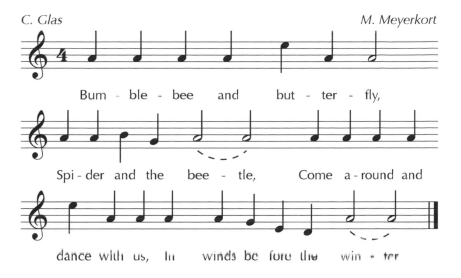

Bum - ble - bee and but - ter - fly,

Spi - der and the bee - tle, Come a - round and

dance with us, In winds be fore the win - ter

2. Bumblebee of summertime,
   Do once more your best,
   Hum around and dance with us,
   Before your winter's rest.

3. Butterfly of summertime,
   Do once more your best,
   Flutter around and dance with us,
   Before your winter's rest.

4. Spider of the summertime,
   Do once more your best,
   Creep around and dance with us,
   Before your winter's rest.

5. Beetle of the summertime,
   Do once more your best,
   Plod around and dance with us,
   Before your winter's rest.

6. Bumblebee and butterfly,
   Spider and the beetle,
   Come now to your Mother Earth,
   And rest there for the winter.

M. Meyerkort   P. Patterson

Wail, wail, wild wind, o - ver wood and town, Let the lit - tle leaves __ dance, let them flut - ter down. _____

2. Fly, fly, swallow blue, fly without a rest,
   In the land of sunshine find a cosy nest.

3. Home, home, beetles all, rain is lashing cold,
   Earth is soft and earth is warm, beetles find your fold.

Autumn winds are sighing,
Stealing through the forest brown,
As they softly pass the tree trunks
Little leaves come falling down.
But a stronger gale is blowing –
Then the leaves themselves
Rise and dance about the forest
Just like little elves.
Faster, faster see them whirling
Till the gale has passed.
One by one the tired leaflets
Sink to rest at last.

We little leaves flutter,
We little leaves sway
Up high on the trees,
Oh this life is most gay;
The sun comes to warm us,
The rain comes to play.

S. Jarman

But I can hear the river calling,
Calling loud and clear;
Stay still a moment one and all,
You too will hear the river's call.

S. Jarman

1. Swinging, swinging, little chestnut cradles,
   Swinging, swinging, in the branches high.
   Rocking, rocking, all the baby chestnuts,
   Rocking, rocking, as the wind flies by.
   Still in the night
   Stars twinkle bright.
   Jack Frost runs soft
   Over fields of white.

2. He nips at the cradles with fingers of ice,
   Down fall the cradles all in a trice.
   Down fall the cradles and split open pop,
   And brown baby chestnuts all out of them hop.
   Down in the warm earth they all sink to rest,
   Sleep, baby chestnuts, on Mother Earth's breast.
   Sleep till the spring sun climbing the skies,
   Shines through the darkness and bids you arise.

In their husks, their shells and clusters,
In their pods, the seeds on high,
Wait to hear the autumn whisper
"Little seeds it's time to fly."
Then they lightly leave their branches
Pop and burst and tumble down,
Hasten, hurry, rush and scurry,
Hide in Mother Earth's warm gown.

J. Mehta

LEAVES

How strong you blow.
Away we go.
Like butterflies
We fly and rise,
We turn around
And then float to the ground.

I am the wind
Do you know what I can do?
I rattle the doors
And the windows, too.
I whistle and shout,
I laugh and I sing,
And then like a bird
I'm off on the wing.

1. In the trees the wind is blowing,
   Hear his nestling song,
   Ooh, ooh, ooh, ooh, ooh!
   All the trees are rocking, swaying,
   When the wind says ooh, ooh, ooh!
   All the trees are rocking, swaying,
   When the wind says ooh!

2. O'er the sea the wind is roaring,
   Blowing up the spray
   Ooh, ooh, ooh, ooh, ooh!
   Hear the waves with mighty thunder,
   When the wind says ooh, ooh, ooh!
   Hear the waves with mighty thunder,
   When the wind says ooh!

LEAVES

Little brothers, little brothers,
Do you hear that song?
The wind is calling,
Loudly calling
Us to join the throng.

S. Jarman

The little winds they whisper, they whisper as they pass.
They tell their tiny secrets to the flowers and the grass.
The big winds go a-buffeting and flustering about.
The little winds whisper, but the big winds SHOUT.

The north wind came along one day,
So strong and full of fun;
He called the leaves down from the trees
And said run, children, run;
They came in red or yellow dress,
In shaded green and brown,
And all the short November day
He chased them round the town.
They ran in crowds, they ran alone,
They hid behind the trees,
The north wind laughing found them there
And called: "No stopping please."
But when he saw them tired out
And huddled in a heap,
He softly said, "Goodnight my dears,
Now let us go to sleep."

Stormwinds send the clouds a-whirling,
Rain comes rushing, swishing, swirling,
Raindrops downwards dance and spatter,
Pitter patter, pitter patter.

S. Jarman

To and fro, to and fro,
Sweeping with my broom I go.
All the fallen leaves I sweep,
In a big and tidy heap.

Acorn, said the old oak tree,
It is time for you to go;
You must say goodbye to me
And fall to the ground below.
There will you lie, buried deep
Under the autumn leaves to sleep,
While around me north winds blow
And the fields are white with snow.
Mother Earth will keep you warm,
Guard you safely from all harm.
Then when you waken, by and by,
A budding twig, so tender, small.
See! Above you near the sky
The forest trees, so strong and tall.
Hear them whisper low and clear,
Welcome! Tiny oak tree dear.

H. Henley

Twinkle, twinkle, little star,
How I wonder what you are!
Art a gateway in the sky?
Art a little angel's eye?
Shine your starry light to earth,
Bring a thousand stars to birth:
Stars in apple, seedpod, pear,
Stars on berries everywhere.
So you guard me near and far-
Twinkle, twinkle, little star.

M. Meyerkort

LATE AUTUMN RING GAME

Song: *Come little leaves – see page 46.*

> *Walk around in open circle formation, clockwise.*
> *Stand still, stretch arms high and imitate falling leaves.*

Winds are blowing all around
Scatter leaves upon the ground.

> *Simple, appropriate gestures.*

So: we put on our hat . . . our coat . . .
our boots . . . we shoulder our rake . . .
and we go into the garden.

> *Walk around in open circle formation, clockwise.*

We rake and rake in autumn weather,
We rake the golden leaves together.
To rake a pile we walk around . . .
A pile of leaves upon the ground.

Someone is coming . . . shush . . .
So hide beneath the bush.
Little steps draw near
And a song I hear.

Song: *My lantern, my lantern – see page 29.*

It is the gnomes . . .
And on each back
Hangs a sack.

> *Get up and have simple, appropriate gestures.*

Trip, trip, trap, trip, trip, trap . . .
Go the gnomes along their track.
Through the caverns make your way,
Find your king as well you may.

Continued...

Put sacks on floor, and stand for the next lines.

Dear king . . . the autumn winds wail,
To sleep goes the snail,
Is there a task for us gnomes
Before we polish the stones?

The king says:
Gather seeds, one and all,
Bring them here, to my hall.

Polishing gesture: for example, hold left hand like a mirror, go with right hand slowly over it, i.e., inside of one hand touching inside of the other hand.

And . . .
Dark is the garden, we will need light,
So we polish and polish our lanterns bright.

Goodbye . . .
With sack and lantern ready,
Our steps are slow and steady.

Place two cupped hands on top of each other for carrying light inside.

Song: *Glimmer, lantern, glimmer – see page 30.*

Use the index finger and thumb of the right hand for picking up seeds, and put them into the cupped left hand.

Here's a seed and there's a seed,
Gather seeds into your sack.
Here's a seed and there's a seed,
Lift them all upon your back.

Song: *Glimmer, lantern, glimmer – see page 30.*

Continued...

Seeds we bring
To our king.
Here a seed and there a seed,
I ay it in the earth to sleep.
Here a seed and there a seed,
Resting through the winter deep.

And . . .

   Quietly stand up.

In the garden, we rake in autumn weather,
We rake the golden leaves together.
To rake a pile we walk around . . .
A pile of leaves upon the ground.

   Walk around in open circle formation.

Gather leaves into a sack,
Lift it well upon your back.

Shake the sack that leaves fall down, leaves fall down.
Cover the compost with leaves so brown, leaves so brown.

   Walk around in open circle formation.

And we shoulder our rake . . .
And we walk home . . .
Rake goes on the hook . . .
Boots go on the mat . . .
Hat . . . and coat on the hook . . .
Now what d'you think of that!

   Quietly sit on the floor.

And at teatime we say to Mummy:
"Listen to my garden-tale:
The sleepy seeds and leaves and snail."

Song: *Come little leaves – see page 46.*

Come little leaves – see page 46.

   Compiled by S. Czemmel

EXTRACTS FROM MICHAELMAS PLAYS

(These are not in sequence.
Adapt one or more extracts to fit the play).

Angel:

    Seeds that glow with heavenly light,
    Take and sow with loving care,
    To Mother Earth that they may grow
    And make of her a garden fair.

Angel:

    I come with the lantern of King Sun
    To bring to everyone
    A little flaming spark
    To lighten winter's dark,
    A little fiery glow
    To warm in winter's snow.
        Take a flaming spark
        To lighten winter's dark,
        Take a fiery glow
        To warm in winter's snow.

Mother Earth:

    Welcome, dear children, from faraway,
    I'm glad you come with me to stay.

Mother Earth:

    Those who tend the earth with care,
    Blessings receive in generous share.

Mother Earth:

    Guard your lantern day and night,
    That you may find the Christ Child's light.

Mother Earth:

    These gifts of summer sun you bring –
    They hide a secret spark.
    Go, find it out and kindle lamps
    And light folk in the dark.

Continued...

Mother Earth:

The fruits of summer sun you bring –
They house a little light,
A little light that glows within,
And warms in winter night.

Mother Earth:

Tend the earth with care
Blessing to be your share.

Flowers, seeds, insects:

Mother dear,
Your children are here.

Mother Earth:

Lie soft and warm
In my arm.

Children:

From heaven high we've come this day,
Dear Mother Earth with you to stay.
We bring a gift with all our love,
A magic seed from heaven above.

Children:

We thank the sun for ripening glow,
The rain and wind that make things grow.
To Mother Earth our thanks we give
For all her fruits whereby we live.

Children:

Dear Mother Earth, you are great, I am small,
Tell me dear Earth, do you know me at all?

Children:

Dear Mother Earth, so great and wise,
Who tends all things with loving care,
We who come from starry skies
Now thank thee for thy gifts so fair.
Uphold our steps, make strong our deeds
And bring to life our magic seeds.

M. Meyerkort & G. Sargeant

M. Meyerkort

N. Foster

1. Gold - en Sun is go - ing down to
   all a - round is dark and still with -

seek his win - ter throne.
in the win - ter night, The

Far and wide the seeds now sleep my
sun will rise with in my heart and

gar - den is a - lone; 2. When
shine a war - mer light.

I am a pumpkin, big and round.
Once upon a time I grew on the ground.
Now I have a mouth, two eyes, a nose.
What are they for, do you suppose?
When I have a candle inside shining bright
I'll be a jack-o'-lantern on Hallowe'en night.

Three little pumpkins, lying very still
In a pumpkin patch on a hill.
This one said, "I'm very green,
But I'll be orange by Hallowe'en."
This one said, "I'm on my way
To be a jack-o'-lantern some day."
This one said, "Oh my, oh my,
Today I'll be a pumpkin pie."

Cut into a pumpkin;
Scoop it with a spoon;
Carve a little mouth
That is shaped like a moon,
Cut two eyes to twinkle,
And a big three-cornered nose.
Use for teeth, ten shiny seeds,
And place them in a row.

Five little goblins on a Hallowe'en night,
Made a very, very spooky sight.
First one danced on his tippy-tip-toes.
The next one tumbled and bumped his nose.
The next one jumped high up in the air.
The next one walked like a fuzzy bear.
The next one sang a Hallowe'en song.
Five goblins played the whole night long!

1. A witch, she went a-shopping
   One October day,
   One October day.
   She bought some stew,
   And a new broom too,
   One fine, clear October day.

2. A witch, she went a-sweeping
   One cleaning day,
   One cleaning day.
   She dusted her house
   And chased out a mouse,
   One busy cleaning day.

3. A witch, she set to stirring
   At suppertime,
   At suppertime.
   She sat down to sup
   And ate it all up,
   At witch's suppertime.

4. A witch, she went to dressing
   One midnight hour,
   One midnight hour.
   She straightened her hat,
   Then patted her cat,
   One late midnight hour.

5. A witch, she went a-riding
   One Hallowe'en night,
   One Hallowe'en night.
   She took up her broom
   And "ALA-KA-ZOOM!"
   One moonlit Hallowe'en night.

A little witch in a pointed cap,
On my door went rap, rap, rap.
When I went to open it,
She was not there;
She was riding on a broomstick,
High up in the air.

1. Here's a witch with a tall, tall hat,
   Two green eyes on a black, black, cat;
   Jack-o'-lanterns in a row,
   Funny clowns are laughing, ho, ho, ho!

2. Bunny's ears flopping up and down,
   Fairy queen wears a fairy crown;
   Gypsy plays a tambourine,
   Cowboy twirls a rope; it's Hallowe'en!

1. A witch once went for a ride on her broom
   Up through the frosty sky.
   She zoomed and zoomed, and she dipped and zipped,
   And she winked at the moon as she passed by,
   At the moon in the frosty sky.

2. She wore a hat that was pointed tall,
   And a cape that was flowing wide,
   And a fierce black cat with a stand up tail
   Rode merrily by her side.
   Rode merrily by her side.

1. Gypsy girls, then a fairy queen,
   Clowns and elves darting in between.
   Here a dashing cowboy,
   There a handsome ploughboy,
   Such a jolly scene,
   This is Hallowe'en.

2. What a night, full of fun and fright!
   Lanterns gleam, all is happy and bright.
   Smiling, bobbing, blinking,
   Jack-o'-lanterns winking,
   What a lively scene,
   This is Hallowe'en.

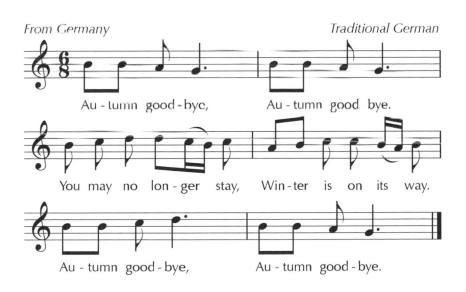

From Germany   *Traditional German*

Au - tumn good - bye,   Au - tumn good bye.

You may no lon - ger stay,   Win - ter is on its way.

Au - tumn good - bye,   Au - tumn good - bye.

Autumn Story

Once there lived a hedgehog called Hedgy Hedgehog. One evening he woke up just as Father Sun was going to bed. Autumn winds were blowing showers of golden, red and brown leaves across the meadow.

Hedgy Hedgehog scrambled out of his bed under the hedge and began to look for worms and beetles. As he trotted along he mumbled to himself: "All I need is a few worms and beetles to eat. I am getting nice and fat. Soon I will make myself a nest and lie down for my winter rest."

Hark! Who was that calling? Was it Mother Earth calling her children? Already many beetles and butterflies were nestling amongst the leaves and grasses. Autumn had come.

Hedgy Hedgehog began to look around for a soft bed of leaves. Above the hedge the sky was grey and wintry. "I'll stay here," he said to himself. He crawled into his leafy bed and curled up ready to go to sleep for the winter.

Busybody Squirrel Nutkin was still busy searching for nuts. When he heard Mother Earth calling he said: "Wait, Mother Earth. I'll go to sleep when it gets really cold."

He scurried down the tree and sat on the grass beneath, looking for nuts. "I have to collect lots more nuts and acorns," he said. He put some into his cheeks and carried them up the tree. Two of his store cupboards were already full so he put them into a new hiding place. Then he sat on a branch looking about him. What a lovely brown coat he had.

Mother Earth called again, "Squirrel Nutkin, Squirrel Nutkin." And the wind sang a song for him:

> Squirrel Nutkin has a coat of brown,
> The loveliest coat in woodland town.
> Two bright eyes look round to see
> Where the sweetest nuts may be.

Squirrel Nutkin held up his two tufted ears and listened. Then he darted away and was gone amongst the branches.

B. Marking

The Giant Turnip

Once upon a time Grandfather planted a turnip seed. "Grow, my turnip," he said, "grow and become big. Grow and become firm and sweet."

The turnip grew and grew. It grew and became firm and sweet. It grew and became big, and bigger. It became a giant turnip.

"It is time to pull up the turnip," said Grandfather. He took hold of the turnip and he pulled and pulled, but the turnip would not budge.

Grandfather called Grandmother to help him pull up the turnip. Grandmother held onto Grandfather, Grandfather took hold of the turnip and they pulled and pulled, but the turnip would not budge.

Grandmother called Grandchild to help pull up the turnip. Grandchild held onto Grandmother, Grandmother held onto Grandfather, Grandfather took hold of the turnip and they pulled and pulled, but the turnip would not budge.

Grandchild called the dog to help pull up the turnip. The dog held onto Grandchild, Grandchild held onto Grandmother, Grandmother held onto Grandfather, Grandfather took hold of the turnip and they pulled and pulled but the turnip would not budge.

The dog called the cat to help pull up the turnip. The cat held onto the dog, the dog held onto Grandchild, Grandchild held onto Grandmother, Grandmother held onto Grandfather, Grandfather took hold of the turnip and they pulled and pulled, but the turnip would not budge.

The cat called the mouse to help pull up the turnip. The mouse held onto the cat, the cat held onto the dog, the dog held onto Grandchild, Grandchild held onto Grandmother and Grandmother held onto Grandfather, Grandfather took hold of the turnip, and they pulled and pulled . . . . . and whoops out it came!

From Russia

The Autumn Blanket

Mother Earth was sitting in her cosy red room under the roots of the fig tree. Her fingers were busy weaving, in and out, they were weaving an autumn blanket for her children – an autumn blanket to keep them warm when the days grew cold.

In and out, her fingers went. In and out, an autumn blanket to keep out the cold.

Mother Earth wove many things into her blanket: pink and brown grasses, golden corn sheaves, white woolly clouds and red-tipped leaves. In and out, an autumn blanket to keep out the cold.

After many days of work the weaving was finished and Mother Earth put it down. She settled into her chair and fell asleep.

In the night sky the stars were twinkling. They looked through the roots of the fig tree into the red room where Mother Earth was sleeping. They saw the autumn blanket with its pink and brown grasses, its golden corn sheaves, its white woolly clouds and its red-tipped leaves – all woven together, in and out, to keep out the cold.

"A warm blanket indeed." the stars agreed. "But where are the lights to guide the earth children through the winter nights? Winter will be dark. Let us give them some of our light."

Mother Earth was dreaming of twinkling stars, and when she awoke she found beams of starlight woven into her autumn blanket. It sparkled out of berry and seedpod, out of apple and pear.

Mother Earth smiled and rose from her chair. Now the autumn blanket was ready. It had both warmth and light for her children to wear through the cold and through the dark. And so she took the blanket and spread it out over the land.

S. Perrow

The Little Grey Pony

There was once a man who owned a little grey pony. Every morning, when the birds were singing, the man would jump on his pony and ride away, clippety, clippety, clap! The man rode to town and to country, to church and to market, uphill and down hill; and, one day, he heard something fall with a clang on a stone in the road. Looking back, he saw a horseshoe lying there. And when he saw it, he cried:

> "What *shall* I do? What *shall* I do?
> My little grey pony has lost a shoe!"

Then down he jumped in a great hurry and looked at one of the pony's forefeet, but nothing was wrong. He lifted the other forefoot, but the shoe was still there. He examined one of the hind-feet, and began to think that he was mistaken; but, when he looked at the last foot, he cried again:

> "What *shall* I do? What *shall* I do?
> My little grey pony has lost a shoe!"

Then he made haste to go to the blacksmith, and he called:

> "Blacksmith! Blacksmith! I've come to you;
> My little grey pony has lost a shoe!"

But the blacksmith answered and said:

> "How can I shoe your pony's feet,
> Without some coal the iron to heat?"

So the man left the blacksmith and hurried here and there to buy the coal.

First of all he went to the store, and he said:

> "Storekeeper! Storekeeper! I've come to you;
> My little grey pony has lost a shoe!
> And I want some coal the iron to heat,
> That the blacksmith may shoe my pony's feet."

But the storekeeper answered and said:

> "Now I have apples and candy to sell,
> And more nice things than I can tell;
> But I've no coal the iron to heat,
> That the blacksmith may shoe your pony's feet."

Then the man went away sighing, and saying:

> "What *shall* I do? What *shall* I do?
> My little grey pony has lost a shoe!"

By and by he met a farmer with a wagon, and he said:

> "Farmer! Farmer! I've come to you;
> My little grey pony has lost a shoe!
> And I want some coal the iron to heat,
> That the blacksmith may shoe my pony's feet."

But the farmer answered and said:

> "I've bushels of corn, and hay, and wheat,
> Something for you and your pony to eat;
> But I've no coal the iron to heat,
> That the blacksmith may shoe your pony's feet."

So the farmer drove away and left the man sighing:

> "What *shall* I do? What *shall* I do?
> My little grey pony has lost a shoe!"

But, in the farmer's wagon, the man had seen corn, which made him think of the mill; so he ran to the mill, and called:

> "Miller! Miller! I've come to you;
> My little grey pony has lost a shoe!
> And I want some coal the iron to heat,
> That the blacksmith may shoe my pony's feet."

The miller came to the door in surprise, and he said:

> "I have wheels that go round and round,
> And stones to turn till the grain is ground;
> But I've no coal the iron to heat,
> That the blacksmith may shoe your pony's feet."

Then the man turned away sorrowfully, and sat down on a rock near the roadside, sighing and saying:

> "What *shall* I do? What *shall* I do?
> My little grey pony has lost a shoe!"

After a while a very old woman came down the road, driving a flock of geese to market; and, when she came near the man, she stopped to ask him his trouble. He told her all about it; and, when she had heard it all, she laughed till her geese joined in with a cackle and she said:

> "If you would know where the coal is found,
> You must go to the miner, who works in the ground."

Then the man sprang to his feet, and, thanking the old woman, he ran to the miner. Now the miner had been working many a long day down in the mine, under the ground where it was so dark that he had to wear a lamp on the front of his cap to light him at his work. He had plenty of black coal ready and gave great lumps of it to the man, who took them in haste to the blacksmith.

The blacksmith lighted his great, red fire, and hammered out four fine new shoes, with a cling and a clang. And fastened them on with a rap and a tap! Then away rode the man on his little grey pony – clippety, clippety, clap!

M. Lindsay

M. Lindsay / M. L. Channer   M. L. Channer

What shall I do? What shall I do? My

lit - tle grey po - ny has lost a shoe!

Black - smith! Black - smith! I've come to you.   My

lit - tle grey po - ny has lost a shoe!

How can I shoe your po - ny's feet, With -

out some coal the iron to heat?

Store-keep-er! Store-keep-er! I've come to you;   My

lit - tle grey po - ny has lost a shoe! And I

Continued...

want some coal the iron to heat, That the

black - smith may shoe my po - ny's feet.

Now I have ap-ples and can-dy to sell, And

more nice things than I can tell; But

I've no coal the iron to heat, That the

black - smith may shoe your po - ny's feet.

Far - mer! Far - mer! I've come to you; My

lit - tle grey po - ny has lost a shoe! And I

Continued...

want some coal the iron to heat, That the

black - smith may shoe my po - ny's feet.

I've bush-els of corn, and hay, and wheat,

Some-thing for you and your po - ny to eat; But

I've no coal the iron to heat, That the

black - smith may shoe your po - ny's feet.

Mil - ler! Mil - ler! I've come to you; My

lit - tle grey po - ny has lost a shoe! And I

Continued...

want some coal the iron to heat, That the

black - smith may shoe my po - ny's feet.

I have wheels that go round and round, And

stones to turn till the grain is ground; But

I've no coal the iron to heat, That the

black - smith may shoe your po - ny's feet. If

you would know where the coal is found, You must

go to the mi - ner who works in the ground.

Continued...

I work in the mines where the sun ne-ver shines And

day-light does ne-ver ap - pear＿＿ With my

lamp blaz-ing red on top of my head, In

dan - ger I ne - ver know fear!

Haymaking Song from the Hebridean Islands

From Scotland   *Traditional Scottish*

Chorus

Heel - yew - eel - yo.   Ho - ron - yail - eel

yew - eel - yo.   Hook or - an - yo.   Heel -

Continued...

yew-eel-yo. Ho - ron yail - y. _____

Verse 1 Mi-cha-ël,   Sea - lord,   shield   of light,   to -
Verse 3 Mi-cha-ël,   Sea - lord,   shield   of light,   to -

night   a   boat   puts   out   to sea,   Heel   *(Chorus)*
night   a   child   puts   out   to sea,   Heel   *(Chorus)*

Verse 2 Bro - ken   keel planks   strew   the shore,   so

frail   the boat   so   great   yon sea,   Heel.   *(Chorus)*

This song would not be suitable for young children to sing, but grown-ups may like to sing it for them. The chorus is to be sung at the beginning, and after each verse. The following story for children, Crossing the Sea, was inspired by this song.

Crossing the Sea

There was once a child who lived in a beautiful garden, where happiness reigned and where flowers bloomed with a perfection of scent and colour found nowhere else. The wildest of animals were tame and the lions were as gentle and kind as lambs. This child had many friends among the animals and many other friends: playmates and wise beings who helped him to find the sweetest fruits, or most secretly hidden treasures – the first bird's nest or a dormouse in its winter sleep. One day when the boy was resting after a happy day in the sun, a day of running, jumping and leaping, he said to one of these wise people: "Here everything is so pleasant – is it like this everywhere?"

"No," said the wise one, "there is a country a long way from here, where people are not so happy and where life is hard. There are fewer green fields, and rain and wind blow the trees into crooked shapes. The wind is cold and the sun shines seldom."

"Could it not be as beautiful as this?" asked the child. "Yes," said the wise one, "and the people who live there try to make it more beautiful." – "I am sorry for those people," said the child, "and I wish I could help. Could I not take some of the seeds of the beautiful flowers that grow here and journey to this land and there plant the seeds and tend them? I could help them to catch all the sun when it does shine and shield them from the wind and rain." The wise one pondered and said: "If you are strong enough to make the journey you may go, but you will find the journey hard and you may have to come back before you have done what you wish. But, Godspeed, and you will be welcome back whenever you come."

So the child gathered seeds from his favourite flowers and set off. He had been told in which direction to go as the country was a long way off and he had to cross a sea. He travelled a long way before reaching the sea and had many adventures, saw many things and learnt much. So that by the time he came to the edge of the great sea, he was footsore and weary. The clouds were gathering and a great storm was brewing. The waves were dashing upon the beach and foaming at his feet.

"I cannot go tonight," he said to himself, "I am not ready." But the seeds, still in his pocket, kept most carefully through all his adventures, said:

"If you do not go tonight and plant us as soon as possible, we shall not be able to bloom properly – there is not much time left. Had the sea been calm we should have been in plenty of time – please, try to cross somehow."

So the boy looked around him for a means of crossing the sea. He walked up and down the beach with the waves tearing at the pebbles and shingle and the spray on his face. Very soon he saw a boat – a frail little cockleshell of a boat with the paint peeling off and even one or two holes in it. But the boy remembered the seeds which he had brought and the country to which he was going, and how they would love the bright flowers, but only if he could get them there in time. So he launched the frail little boat on the great sea. It was in danger of being washed back several times. But at last he got it past the breakers and into the sea. Then he rowed onwards. However, the further the little boat got from the shore, the greater were the waves and the stronger the wind. First, to his dismay, one of the oars broke, then, as he endeavoured to row with one oar, on one side then the other, a larger wave than ever came and washed his remaining oar away. The boat sailed on, tossed hither and thither by the waves and wind. By and by, through the mist blown spray, the boy saw dimly the line of another country in the distance – it grew nearer – and then, to his horror, the boy saw it begin to recede again. The wind had changed direction and was blowing against him and the tide also was flowing in a different direction. With the oars gone the little boy could not steer his boat and was dependent upon the wind and the tide. I shall have to go back, thought he. But he remembered the seeds and thought of the new country and new courage woke in his heart. "I will go," said he.

And he dived out of the boat after stowing the seeds away, as carefully as he could, to protect them from sea water. The water was bitterly cold but he struck out manfully, and it seemed to him that instead of growing weaker he grew stronger and could swim more strongly than ever – in fact strangely enough he hardly needed to swim at all but was being borne along. Looking up he saw a great shining warrior in glittering armour astride a horse which was as white as the foam of the sea, with a plumy mane curling like the crest of a wave. The horse was swimming strongly towards the shore, and the warrior on his back, with his sword at his side, looked down on the child and smiled. The boy recognised St. Michaël as his helper and friend and with his aid he reached the beach at last. The great horse found his depth and walked out of the sea onto the wet sand. At the top of the beach, above the cliff, was a wall with a gateway in it. The boy climbed the cliff with some difficulty, but it seemed that someone was calling to him from behind the door, so he made haste. He knocked at the door and slowly it opened. Beyond it he caught a glimpse of the country that needed his flowers so much. Parts of it were dark and heavy, but gleams of sun lit up green fields like those of his home, and he thought: "Somewhere here I must plant my flowers." At that moment he heard the voices of a man and woman, bidding him welcome, and he recognised that these were the voices that had called to him through the door. "We have been waiting for you," said they, "come and take our hands. We will try and help you to find somewhere to plant your flowers."

Though the boy was weak and tired after his long journey he managed, before the gate closed, to turn and wave goodbye to St. Michaël, who had waited to see him safely up the cliff. Then the gate was closed and he turned to his helpers who took him to a little house, where they warmed, dried, and fed him, and then he found places which needed flowers most and planted them there. He was just in time. The seeds germinated and sprouted and by and by their beautiful scented flowers grew. All who passed by, though weary and sad, looked at them and remembered the country from whence they came; and the boy tended them carefully so that when the time came for him to go back they were strong and flourishing.

E. Brooking

Little Ant

Once there lived Little Ant. Yes, Little Ant. One day she was sweeping the floor, and she was sweeping the floor; how she was sweeping the floor. and she found a silver coin. Yes, a silver coin .

Well, she bought yards and yards of blue ribbon. She tied it around her head and she tied it around her waist. And she said, "I do look fine this morning." She went out for a walk and met Bellower the Bull. He was looking over the gate. Then said Bellower the Bull, "My, Little Ant, you do look fine this morning. Will you marry me?" – "First, let me hear your voice," she said. "It's the best voice in the world," said Bellower the Bull. "Moo." – "Oh, it is too loud, I cannot marry you," said Little Ant, putting her fingers in her ears. And off she ran down the lane.

Then she met Gamboling Goat. "My, Little Ant, you look fine this morning. Will you marry me?" - "First let me hear your voice," she said. "It's the best voice in the world," said Gamboling Goat. "Meeeh." – "Oh, it is too loud, I cannot marry you," said Little Ant putting her fingers in her ears. And off she ran down the lane.

Then she met Sniffer the Dog. "My, Little Ant, you look fine this morning. Will you marry me?" – "First let me hear your voice," she said. "It's the best voice in the world," said Sniffer the Dog. "Bow-wow." – "Oh, it is too loud, I cannot marry you," said Little Ant putting her fingers in her ears. And off she ran down the lane.

Then she met Squiggytail the Pig. "My, Little Ant, you look fine this morning. Will you marry me?" – "First let me hear your voice," she said. – "It's the best voice in the world," said Squiggytail the Pig. "Oink." – "Oh, it is too loud, I cannot marry you," said Little Ant putting her fingers in her ears. And off she ran down the lane.

Then she met Catcher the Cat. "My, Little Ant, you look fine this morning. Will you marry me?" – "First let me hear your voice," she said. "It's the best voice in the world," said Catcher the Cat. "Miaow." – "Oh, it is too loud, I cannot marry you," said Little Ant putting her fingers in her ears. And off she ran down the lane.

Then she met Regal Rooster. "My, Little Ant, you look fine this morning. Will you marry me?" – "First let me hear your voice," she said. "It's the best voice in the world," said Regal Rooster. "Cock-a-dodle-doo." – "Oh, it is too loud, I cannot marry you," said Little Ant putting her fingers in her ears. And off she ran down the lane.

When she came to the cornfield she sat down and cried. "Why are you crying?" said Minikin the Mouse. "Everyone has a loud voice and I won't be able to marry," said Little Ant, to which Minikin the Mouse replied: "I have the softest voice in the world. Listen: Ee." Then Little Ant was happy and Minikin the Mouse and Little Ant were married, and they danced among the cornstalks.

From Spain.

The Kite

Once upon a time there was a boy whose father helped him make a kite. They worked on it in the winter, until its wooden cross was surrounded by transparent paper of yellow, red and blue.

In the summer the boy flew his kite and the sun was so pleased with its colours that he sent his clearest rays of light. And so the kite looked like a flaming cross in the sky. The boy let his kite rise as high as it could until the string came to an end and the kite could go no farther.

Whoosh! There came a gust of wind. The string snapped and the kite went flying into the sky. The boy saw it rise higher and higher. Soon the kite had gone so high that he could barely see it.

Up there in the blue there was much to be seen. First the kite saw a crow.

"Good morning," croaked the crow.

"Good morning," replied the kite.

"Are you a bird, with your flaming wings and long tail?"

"No, I am not a bird."

"What are you then and from whence do you come?"

"I come from the lad standing down there; he made me himself."

"And where are you going?"

"That I do not know. I want to fly into the sky."

"Then you do not belong here. Up here every being knows whence he comes and whither he goes. I fly every winter to the south, and every summer to the north. I advise you to return to the human beings below, for if you do not know where you are going, you will lose your way in heaven." But the kite was determined and rose further into the heights.

Then the kite met a seed.

"Good day," whispered the seed.

"Good day," replied the kite.

"Are you also a seed with your roots and shoots?"

"Not I."

"Where are you going?"

"I do not know. I want to travel into heaven."

"Then you do not belong here. Up here everyone knows where he is going. I sail through the air and take in that which moves from the east to the west – the warmth of the sun. When I have taken it into myself, I travel down again and bring it to the earth. The earth then lets a flower grow out of me. If you do not know what to do, I advise you to descend to the earth or you will lose your way in these heights." But the kite did not hear and soared higher.

Then he glided past a cloud.

"Good evening," murmured the cloud.

"Good evening," said the kite.

"Are you a cloud with your flaming sunset red?" asked the cloud.

"No, I was made by human beings. I came from the boy down there."

"And where are you going?"

"Oh, only into the sky."

"Then you do not belong here. Everyone here knows his purpose. I collect the last red of the sunset and turn it into the red of the sunrise. I rain down with the red of the sunrise and bless the earth and when I have done that the sun carries me up once more, so that the red of the sunrise can again be made. And so I travel up and down. I advise you to go back to the boy, for without a goal you will lose your way up here." But the kite would not return and rose higher.

Then he came to the stars.

"Good night," sang the stars.

"Good night," sang the kite with them.

"What news do you bring to us, you comet of the earth?" sang the stars.

"I come from the boy who lies sleeping down there on the earth," said the kite. "He is waiting until I return but in the meantime he has fallen asleep, and is dreaming about me."

"We ask you to take our blessings back to the boy," sang the stars and every one of them gave the kite some of their light.

Then came the Angel Michaël. He took a star and hurled it towards the strange newcomer. The kite burst into flames and like a torch plunged into the depths.

The boy awoke from a dream. But when he looked around he realised that it could not have been an ordinary dream for next to him lay the cross of his kite and the coloured paper had been devoured by flames.

And the cross was no longer wooden but was of bright, heavenly iron. The boy was astounded when he saw that. But he was also vexed because his beautiful kite was gone.

At home his father comforted him: "Let us be glad. If your kite was not burnt you would never have received this cross of heavenly iron. This iron is lighter than the lightest wood and stronger than the strongest steel. Let us use it to make a new kite."

This they did. And next summer when the kite rose to the heavens he again met those who travelled from north to south, from east to west and from heaven to earth. And when he came to the stars he again met Michaël and again he plunged burning to the earth. But the cross of heavenly iron shone even more brightly than before.

And this happened for many years and with every year the cross became brighter and stronger. And when the boy had grown up the cross took on a different form: it turned into a shining sword which gleamed with the light of the stars. With this sword the growing man travelled through the world and he became a knight and servant of Michaël.

U. de Haes

Recommended Reading

A is for Ox, B. Sanders ISBN 9780679417118 Pantheon Books
Failure to Connect, J. Healy, Simon & Schuster
Set Free Childhood, M. Large ISBN 9781903458433 Hawthorn Press
Rudolf Steiner, R. Lissau ISBN 9781903458563 Hawthorn Press
Lifeways, G. Davy & B. Voors ISBN 9780950706245 Hawthorn Press
The Spiritual Tasks of the Homemaker, M. Schmidt-Brabant
    ISBN 9780904693843 Temple Lodge Publishing, England
Education Towards Freedom ISBN 9780863156519
    Floris Press, Edinburgh, Scotland
Work and Play in Early Childhood, F. Jaffke
    ISBN 9780863152276 Floris Books
Festivals, Family and Food, D. Carey & J. Large
    ISBN 9780950706238 Hawthron Press
Festivals Together, S. Fitzjohn, M. Weston & J. Large
    ISBN 9781869890469 Hawthorn Press
Understanding Children's Drawings, M. Strauss ISBN 9781855841994
    Rudolf Steiner Press, England
The Wisdom of Fairytales, R. Meyer ISBN 9780863152085 Floris Books
A Guide to Child Health, M. Glöckler & W. Goebel
    ISBN 9780863159671 Floris Books
Education as Preventive Medicine – A Salutogenic Approach,
    M Glöckler, Rudolf Steiner College Press, California, USA.
Between Form and Freedom, B Staley ISBN 9781903458891 Hawthorn Press
Brothers and Sisters, K. König, Floris Books
The Challenge of the Will, Margret Meyerkort & Rudi Lissau,
    Rudolf Steiner College Press
The Oxford Nursery Songbook,
    ISBN 9780193301931 Oxford University Press
The Oxford Dictionary of Nursery Rhymes
    ISBN 9780198600886 Oxford University Press

Let us Form a Ring,
    WECAN Waldorf Early Childhood Association of North America
The Book of 1000 Poems ISBN 9780001855083
    HarperCollins Children's Books
English Fairy Tales, J. Jacobs
The Complete Grimm's Fairy Tales ISBN 9780394709307 Random House
Milly Molly Mandy Books, J. Lankester Brisley, Puffin Books
Seven-Year-Old Wonder Book, I. Wyatt ISBN 9780863159435 Floris Books

Acknowledgements

Further to the acknowledgement on page 3 of this book, the following is a list of permissions granted to reproduce previously published copyright material. Where it has not been possible to locate the original copyright holder, we tender our apologies to any owner whose rights may have been unwittingly infringed.

Yellow the Bracken titled Autumn – by Florence Hoatson, reprinted by kind permission of Chambers Harrap Publishers Ltd. *To and fro, to and fro,* from This Little Puffin, published by Penguin Books. From HarperCollins Publishers Ltd, we are grateful to reproduce the following items from The Book of 1000 Poems: *Miller, miller,* by Ivo O. Eastwick; *Farmer, is the harvest ready – titled Bread –* by H. E. Wilkinson, and *The Harvest,* by Alice C. Henderson. *Spindle wood, spindle wood – titled Alms in Autumn –* from a poem by Rose Fyleman and reproduced with permission from The Society of Authors as the literary representative of the Estate of Rose Fyleman.

Wynstones Press

Wynstones Press publishes and distributes a range of books, including many titles for children, parents and teachers.

Also available is a wide selection of postcards, folded cards and prints reproduced from original work by a variety of artists. Included amongst these are many works by David Newbatt, who illustrated the covers for this book.

Wynstones Press also distributes a selection of beautifully illustrated Advent Calendars, from publishers in Europe.

For further information please contact:

Wynstones Press
Ruskin Glass Centre
Wollaston Road
Stourbridge
West Midlands DY8 4HE.
England.

Telephone: +44 (0) 1384 399455
Email: info@wynstonespress.com
Website: wynstonespress.com